The 8 Limbs of Yoga Journal

By

Beth Daugherty, M.S., M.A., E-RYT, RCYT

The 8 Limbs of Yoga Journal
By Beth Daugherty

Copyright © 2016 Beth Daugherty

All rights reserved, including the right of reproduction in whole or in part in any form. Reproduction of this work in any form; electronic, mechanical, or other means, now known or later invented, is forbidden without written consent of the author/publisher.

DISCLAIMER: This book does not provide medical advice, and the information in this book should not be considered as medical advice. The content of this book is in no way intended to be a substitute for professional medical advice, diagnosis, or treatment, or a substitute for the guidance of an experienced yoga teacher. The information provided in this book is for informational use only and meant to be used as a basis for discussion with your doctor and yoga teacher only. Always get your doctor's permission before beginning a yoga practice, especially if you have an injury or medical condition. Always inform your yoga teacher of your injury or ailment so that he or she can provide guidance and recommend modifications for certain postures. The publisher, the author, or any third parties mentioned in this publication are not liable for any damages—to include, but not be limited to, incidental and consequential damage, personal injury, wrongful death, lost profits, or damages resulting from employment or business interruption—resulting from the correct or incorrect use or inability to use the information contained in this book. By purchasing and utilizing this book, you are agreeing to these terms of use. If you do not agree to the above terms, please do not use this book.

ISBN -13: 978-0-9970197-1-1

Media

Lifespan Yoga® is a registered trademark to Beth Daugherty, founder of Lifespan Yoga®, LLC.

Other Books by Beth Daugherty:

Nikita's Sun (2012)

Lifespan Yoga®: Developmental Psychology Meets the Practice and Teaching of Yoga (2014)

Gentle Yoga: A Lifespan Yoga® Introduction (2015)

Chair Yoga: Lifespan Yoga® for Health and Wellness (2015)

Sign up for news about classes, workshops, speaking and books at
WWW.LIFESPANYOGA.COM

View gentle yoga videos on the Lifespan Yoga® YouTube Channel.

A Note from Beth

What if a tree had just one limb? It would look quite sad. So it is with yoga. Practicing just one limb of yoga and missing out on the other seven can feel incomplete and unbalanced. Yoga is an eight limb system with each limb giving strength and stability to the others, just as the limbs of a tree do. The eight limb yoga system is what makes yoga so accessible to all people from every country around the planet.

This guided journal is designed to give structure to your personal transformation and help you write your yoga story. I originally designed this guided journal for my yoga students and found they not only like to write, but they also like to make lists, doodle, draw, sketch, scribble, paint, collage and use every art technique known to man to get their thoughts and ideas on paper. I hope this journal can also be a project, a scrapbook, an art journal and a storage place for the insights you gain along your yoga journey.

The questions I ask here are simply a jumping off point. There is no order. For example, many people come to yoga through the third limb, postures, so this may be where they begin this journal. Or, if it is your style, work through the questions one by one in order. It may be fun to work on this journal with a friend or in a training group. This creative exploration of your yoga practice will take you exactly where you need to go.

Yoga students are in the habit of self-development so it makes sense you will continue to change, develop and improve all through the life span. Have a wonderful time exploring, swinging and hanging off the eight limbs.

Table of Contents

The First Limb of Yoga 9

    Nonviolence (Ahimsa) 11

    Truth telling (Satya) 23

    Nonstealing (Asteya) 35

    Managing Your Self (Bramacharya) 59

    Nonpossessiveness (Aparigraha) 69

The Second Limb of Yoga 75

    Purity (Saucha) 77

    Contentment (Santosha) 81

    Discipline (Tapas) 85

    Self-Study (Svadhyaya) 95

    Surrender (Ishvara Pranidhana) 101

The Third Limb: Yoga Postures 107

    Gentle Standing Poses 107

    Gentle Balance Poses 111

    Gentle Prone Poses 112

    Gentle Seated and Twisting Postures 116

    Gentle Supine Poses and Backbends 119

    Gentle Inversions 121

The Fourth Limb: Energy of Life 123

The Fifth Limb: Withdrawal 129

The Sixth Limb: Concentration 137

The Seventh Limb: Meditation 143

The Eighth Limb: Bliss 145

About the Author 149

The First Limb of Yoga

This section of the journal is dedicated to your thoughts and reflections on the five core ethical principles of yoga (*yamas*). This first limb is also known as the social disciplines, or restraints, of yoga. These specific ethical principles are all about the people and relationships we are surrounded by in our day to day life. As you are writing, think about your loved ones, your family and friends.

Do not stop there. Think about strangers, politicians, teachers, and people from all walks of life swirling around you. What are your values? Does your behavior with other people reflect those values? Are your relationships a model of those personal ethics and values? The ethical principles of yoga prompt a deeper reflection of what you actually value, think and do.

Draw the first limb here:

Nonviolence (Ahimsa)

The first ethical principle of ahimsa, nonviolence, guides yogis to avoid violence and practice compassion to all beings, including the self. This begins with not harming other living beings. What do you think about this practice?

Why did the masters believe this is a social discipline?

Describe what violence means to you and how you feel in a violent situation.

Gandhi said nonviolence was the most radical act and a great risk. This makes yogis serious radicals! We are at odds with the violence all around us and the goal is to practice compassion to others and to ourselves. When we begin, it seems impossible as we are confronted over and over with situations in our normal life that stir up aggression. How do you resist violence?

What does compassion mean to you?

Can a person be nonviolent but not compassionate? Describe such a situation.

What does compassion to all beings mean to you?

How do you demonstrate compassion?

The ethical principle of nonviolence guides yogis to practice compassion to the self. This includes simple things like getting enough sleep, exercise, and eating a proper diet but it also is about how you speak to yourself and how you think about yourself. What do you think?

Describe your sleep. Consider if it is deep, long and restful.

Describe your exercise routines.

Describe your diet. Include if you need to make changes and if you have had struggles with your diet or food.

If you have a prayer practice, describe it here.

If you have a meditation practice, describe it here.

What do you need to change in your life?

Describe a balanced life for you.

What happens when you do something that scares you?

What things do you do that are brave?

At times it can take a lot of courage to take care of our needs and say no to others. What have you done lately that was courageous?

The refugee crisis is all over the news. How would nonviolence look in this situation?

Describe a time where you felt compassion toward others and you knew you were living the ethical principle of nonviolence.

What will you do today that demonstrates your compassion towards others?

Describe your environment. Are some spaces you live or work compassionate and some less so?

List the problems you run into when you practice compassion.

Describe a time you felt another person or organization put a halt to your compassionate acts.

Do you think governments are large organizations that halt compassionate acts?

Some violence can be rooted in fear. What is the difference between fear and just unfamiliar?

Sometimes we are violent towards another by simply trying to control them or fix them. Are you a fixer?

Are you a control freak? What kinds of things do you feel compelled to control?

If you focus on fixing or controlling others, you could be avoiding fixing your own problems. Describe a time when you may have done this.

Nonviolence includes our actions toward other living beings; as a consequence, some yogis are vegetarian or vegan. What do you think about this idea?

Describe your relationship with animals.

Are you a vegetarian or would you like to be? Why or Why not?

The advanced practice of nonviolence is to eliminate violent thoughts and words. List all your violent thoughts.

List violent words that run through your head.

Describe how you avoid negative actions.

A famous author once said we are all in this leaky boat called earth together. Our fortunes are correlated. What do you think?

One of the most dangerous and persistent negative thoughts we have about other people is discrimination. Hating others due to some perceived difference is considered negative thinking. What do you think?

Do you have thoughts about who should and should not do yoga that may be discriminatory? Who and why?

Describe how you avoid hurtful discrimination.

Describe a time you moved your thoughts from destructive to productive and peaceful.

As we advance our practice and work to avoid negative actions and negative thoughts, do we naturally become more compassionate? How can this happen?

Practicing nonviolence changes our thoughts and our behavior. After all this journaling what are your thoughts about nonviolence now? Write a prayer, poem or song lyrics that sum it all up for you.

Truth telling (Satya)

The ethical principle of honesty (satya) begins with telling the truth. Why is this good for others if you practice it?

Why did the masters believe this is a social discipline?

So to state the obvious--Do you lie? What type of lies do you tell?

Use this space to illustrate, doodle or collage a lie.

What lies have you told to yourself or to others?

Do you lie to your children? Do you lie about your children?

Describe lies told in business.

List lies customers are told.

What lies do you tell your parents, spouse, or friends?

Describe a time you were caught lying.

Some say it is hard or dangerous to tell the truth. Why do you lie?

This ethical principle in yoga also includes not deceiving others in our thoughts, words and actions. Sometimes we know our words are literally true, but do we really need to let everyone know? Why do we do this?

When you say *yes* to one thing, you may be saying *no* to something else. If you do not want to do the thing you said yes to, it is a lie. Describe a time you experienced this.

Keeping a promise is an honest act and fair to others, but it is also being good to yourself. How do you keep your promises to yourself?

How do you keep your promises to others?

Describe a nice person.

Do you think you should be a certain type of nice?

Insincere behavior is not genuine and is considered dishonest. It is an advanced practice in yoga to let go of pretenses and not be fake. Illustrate what is fake to you.

Being fake is a lie. Do you pretend you are something you are not?

Sometimes it is good to keep quiet about something and sometimes keeping a secret is dishonest. Describe something you keep quiet that maybe you should start talking about to be more honest with others.

Another common behavior that hurts others is denial. Sometimes it may be necessary to deny the truth so we can get through the day. Often though, facing up to a truth is more honest, especially if others are hurt by your denial. What do you think? Are you in denial?

Discuss family and friends you have known that were in denial and how that impacted all the people around them.

We are surrounded by others' unjust behavior. Describe a situation where a crime was committed and no one spoke up and why this hurts others.

How do you balance your political beliefs and the dishonesty in politics?
Are you an activist? If possible, do you vote?

How do you silence yourself?

Procrastination is a lie about time. Do you lie to yourself about time?

Some people say the most selfish person in the room is the one who walks in late. Describe what happens when one person is late and how that can impact a group.

How do you procrastinate? Do you think you have more time than you really do? Do you procrastinate at home but not at work, lying in one environment and not the other? Why do you procrastinate in one place and not the other?

Sometimes putting into practice the combination of the first two ethical principles of yoga, truth telling and nonviolence, can be tricky. When telling the truth is hurtful to another, the practice suggests yielding to nonviolence and compassion for the other. How do you do this?

It is also considered an advanced practice to let go of strong opinions. How do you let go of always voicing strong opinions?

List ways you can speak more carefully.

What do you think about all this? What is your understanding of the topic now? Draw or write a prayer, poem, affirmation, picture or song lyrics that sums it all up for you.

Illustrate an example of a truth for you.

Nonstealing (Asteya)

Define what stealing means to you and draw it if you like.

What did you learn about stealing when you were young?

Describe a time you took something you did not need.

What about your parents; did they ever steal? How did you feel about that?

Describe the opposite of stealing. How does that connect to the last ethical principle of honesty?

Why did the masters believe this is a social discipline?

List things that you own that you hold on to and will not let go.

Comparing yourself to others all the time is stealing your own opportunity to be who you were meant to be. How does this hurt the community?

List things that make you feel cheated.

Talk about a time you felt superior to others and ask yourself if it was true?

A person who is arrogant can be stealing everyone else's feelings of worthiness. How have you been arrogant?

How do you steal from the earth?

How do you steal from the future?

What types of behaviors do you have that may cause you to lose your own opportunities? How do you steal from yourself?

How do you place too many demands on yourself?

If you place too many expectations on yourself, you are stealing your own peace and joy, and probably the peace of those around you. What do you think about this?

If you self-sabotage you are stealing your own potential successes. Why is this a social discipline?

If you do not believe in yourself, you are stealing the possibility of doing something wonderful. Describe a situation in which you didn't believe in yourself. What do you think you lost by not believing in yourself?

Describe your self-esteem right now.

How do you judge yourself?

I had a student who said she spent seventy percent of the day criticizing herself for being fat. What runs through your head that steals your thoughts and your joy?

Many of us are perfectionists. How do you demand perfection from yourself and how does that impact others?

Describe how thinking about and living in the past can impact the people you are surrounded by in this moment. How do those people feel?

If you are waiting to do something because something else has to happen first, are you living in the present or the future? How does this impact your loved ones? Do they feel like you are stealing their ability to live in the now?

List everything going on in this moment, this day, and this week. Do you take time to reflect on what is going on right now?

Think about money. Are you a good steward of your money? How so, or why not?

Do you try to educate yourself about money and investments? If not, what's holding you back?

Being good with money today gives you a better chance of having some tomorrow. Do you steal from the future with debt or overspending?

Are you generous with the money you do have?

The advanced yoga practice is living with integrity by being a good steward of time and money. Describe someone you know that lives with integrity.

Do you feel life is fair?

Are you dissatisfied with your life?

When you take things, describe how you may give something back.

How do you try to make things fair?

What do you have in excess?

Describe the feeling of having too many clothes in your closet.

Where may there be too much furniture in the house?

List all the things you are grateful for:

Describe all the ways you say thank you.

Give an example of a time you focused on what you don't have and what happened. Did anything change?

How do you feel abundance?

Do you look back in time and feel gratitude for those that came before you? Who and Why?

Do you know about and understand the hardships they faced in their lives?

What possibilities in your life make you excited?

How do you create yourself?

What is it like to lust after someone else's possessions?

Describe how you could get sidetracked from your own dreams.

Think about your close relationships. Do you ever try to control or manipulate others to boost yourself? Who and Why?

Have you ever "one upped" one of your friends' stories? How do you think this made them feel?

How do you steal someone's space with all your stuff?

Do you pay attention to others or do you steal their time by ignoring them when they want to be involved in activities or conversations?

Describe someone who steals everyone's time by causing lots of drama and making situations about them. How do you get away from these people?

Describe a person that steals time by dragging everyone down with them when they are down. Have you ever done this?

List all the ways a sarcastic person can steal joy from others.

Talk about how being supportive can reduce stealing the time and joy of others.

How can you lift people up? Do people feel uplifted when they're with you?

Do you think people feel like something has been taken away from them when they are with you? Their time or joy?

Describe how listening to people is the opposite of stealing time or joy. Do you listen to people?

List all the compliments you would like to give someone close to you.

How does complaining steal the moment for you and others?

Think about your skills, work, hobbies and career. How do you grow your competence in these areas?

A skillful and competent person does not have to use others, live off of others or steal from others. They will contribute rather than take way. Describe how you develop yourself so that you do not have to steal from others.

I admit I am a bit of a dreamer. How does sitting around hoping and wishing steal time?

If at work or home you pretend you have skills you do not, how does this steal from the people you were dishonest to?

How do you spend time on your craft/expertise?

Are you available to get what you want or are you always running around like a chicken with its head cut off?

How do you find mentors? How do you then avoid becoming a burden to your mentor(s) once you have found them?

Have mentors or bosses stolen from you by unfair work conditions? How did this happen?

In what circumstances do you want more than you need (materially and also in non-material ways like attention and recognition)?

The advanced practice is letting go of the desire and even thoughts about taking things. Where are you with this?

What do you think about this? Define what non-stealing now means to you and write a prayer, poem, affirmation, song lyrics or draw it. How does this come together for you?

Managing Your Self (Bramacharya)

The ethical principle of managing your personal energy is about finding balance. Many people think this principle is only about sexual energy and maintaining celibacy, but a modern interpretation includes all sense pleasures. There are many areas where humans can overdo it or underdo it, not just sex. Why is this good for others if you practice it?

Why did the masters believe this is a social discipline?

Do you feel pleasure and not addiction doing your favorite thing?

Describe something you have an addiction to and how it makes you feel.

Why do you move past the place of "just enough", into excess or overdoing it?

Do you overdo it with food? When?

Do you overdo it with work? Under what circumstances?

Do you overdo it with exercise, yoga, dance, running? Are you stealing from someone else when you do so? Do you balance the time out in some way with that person?

Energy management is one of the foundations of the yoga practice. Our personality type, introvert or extrovert, helps us understand ourselves. Do you know your personality type?

When you are restless, what calms you?

When you are down, what brings you up?

Are the things that calm you or bring you up healthy? If not, what healthy things can you replace them with?

What is your excess? Pick your poison. Overeating? Drinking too much? Smoking? Pills or other drugs?

Energy management includes moderation and eliminating compulsions.

What kinds of things are you greedy for?

Do you begin the day ready to indulge?

Do you feel miserable and hung over when you overdo it?

Do you overdo material possessions?

Do you fast? Under what circumstances? How does this make you feel?

Are you celibate? By choice? Or would you like to have a healthy sexual relationship? What's keeping you from trying to find the right person?

Are you abstinent from any substance?

Think about sleep. Do you know how much sleep is enough for your body? What things do you adjust in your life to get more rest when you need it?

Describe the food, rest, exercise and recreation needs that must be met in order for you to feel "in balance / balanced".

Do you feel energetic when you wake up?

How does energy management enhance the sacredness of living?

How do you honor everyone as sacred?

Do you honor yourself as sacred? Under what circumstances do you struggle to do this?

How can you cherish life?

Do you regularly challenge your own boundaries, expand your capabilities and skills? How?

Do you feel life is sacred?

Do you enter the day with a sense of holiness?

What kinds of things make you feel passionate?

How does managing your personal energy enhance your vitality?

List what makes you come alive?

Do you waste energy chatting and talking about nothing?

Where does your energy leak out?

A sense of wonder is natural. How frequently do you go to bed with a sense of accomplishment?

Do you go to bed with a sense of wonder?

Do you live with peace?

Do you take full responsibility for your relationships?

Do you regard all other human beings with respect?

Do you take sexual responsibility in your relationship? Do you protect yourself?

The advanced practice is complete elimination of addictions, and having no desire to seek addictive substances. Do you think if we remove an addiction we find balance, love for self and love for others?

What do you think about this? What is your understanding of the topic now? Draw or write a prayer, poem, affirmation, picture or song lyrics that sums it all up for you.

Nonpossessiveness (Aparigraha)

The ethical principle of non-possessiveness is about letting go and especially letting go of greed. It includes reducing what you want and becoming non-attached. Why is this good for others if you practice it?

Why did the masters believe this is a social discipline?

What things or people make you feel possessive?

Has anyone ever called you a possessive or greedy person? How do you think you can let go of your possessiveness?

The ethical principle of nonpossessiveness includes not wanting more than you need. Do you dream about having things that are not yours?

Do you lust after someone else's accomplishments?

Do you covet people's things or relationships you do not have?

Aparigraha also includes jealousy. Are you jealous? How? Of who?

Who are you holding on to?

One great way to practice is letting go. What is it time to let go of?

Do you need to let go of things or people?

Do you have too much?

What are you clinging to?

This discipline includes is letting go of ideas that are no longer useful. Do you need to let go of ideas that you have grown out of?

What are some outdated ideas you have about your career or family duties?

Are you still hanging onto discrimination about other races or ethnic groups?

Make a list of any negative people in your life?

Letting go of things that no longer work, no longer serve us or are no longer useful frees up a lot of physical and psychological space. Do you need to let go of religions or beliefs that no longer make sense to you?

After letting go there may be emptiness, then creativity rushes in. How are you creative?

What creativity explodes when you let go?

The advanced practice is generosity. What do you think about this?

What do you think about this? What is your understanding of the topic now? Draw or write a prayer, poem, affirmation, picture or song lyrics that sums it all up for you.

The Second Limb of Yoga

The following questions are designed for you to reflect on personal disciplines (*niyamas*). These are positive individual actions, habits, behaviors and states of mind yogis can cultivate every day for the entire life span. There is no age where we no longer need personal discipline. These timeless principles are positive and build internal strength.

To gain any sort of happiness or contentment, modern psychologists encourage you to get a hold of your consciousness and be in control of the mind. This is one of the main training processes in yoga.

Psychologists call optimal experience the moments when all the stars line up in an experience and we feel like a master of our future. We make these happen through focus and hard work, pushing ourselves to places we did not know we could go. I see this look in the faces of young graduates who have done a great job in training; they are confident and proud the moment they are handed that certificate. They know they did it, it was hard work and they have changed because of it.

Purity (Saucha)

The personal discipline of purity can bring up ideas of the perfect diet, lovely disposition and a polished image. Really it is an exercise in cleanliness of body, mind, home, and other surroundings you may find yourself in. It is not just about showering and smelling good, it includes letting go of what is unnecessary, eliminating bad habits, and becoming free from material attachments.

What does purity mean to you? Give examples from your own life.

What does cleanliness mean to you?

Give examples of how you define clean and dirty.

What does it mean to purify your thoughts?

Thinking about the concept of subtraction, what can you take away that will make things clean?

What can you take away that will make you feel free?

The advanced practice is being able to easily discriminate the good from bad, and being able to let go of the bad with ease. List any bad things you want to eliminate in your life:

What does simple living mean to you? Give examples in your own life.

What do you think about this? What is your understanding of the topic now? Draw or write a prayer, poem, affirmation, picture or song lyrics that sums it all up for you.

Contentment (Santosha)

The personal discipline of contentment is about satisfaction with what we have and gratitude. Not worrying is part of this practice because we live in the moment, not in an unknown future. The advanced practice is contentment even in the storm or when people are against you. This group of journal questions covers happiness, satisfaction with your daily life, even the weather and the part of the country you live in. Let's get started!

List everything that makes you happy.

How are you satisfied with your relationships?

How are you satisfied with life in general?

How are you content with your work?

How are you satisfied with your home?

What makes you happy in your home?

Do you know anyone who always complains about the weather? Are you content with the weather where you live?

Why are you satisfied with the part of the country you live in?

Why would you want to move?

Are you satisfied with your local politics? What drives you mad about politics?

Are you content with the environment around you?

What is your understanding of the topic now? Draw or write a prayer, poem, affirmation, picture or song lyrics that sums it all up for you.

Discipline (Tapas)

The personal discipline of *tapas* is about transformation. *Tapas* is a practice of balanced austerity, sacrifice, and discipline. What do these three things mean to you?

Are you consistent in striving toward your goals? List a few goals and rate your consistency with each.

What is your one true goal?

Do you go after the goal with joy?

Are you non-attached as you go for your goals?

Describe an austere person. What do you think of when someone says austerity?

How do you think austerity and strong character go together?

What is your yoga goal? Is it self-realization? Enlightenment? Union of God and Self?

Many yogis talk about using heat and fire to burn up the stuff you do not like (think of burning off the calories). *Tapas* and fire go together; why?

Tapas and discipline go together, why?

Do you think discipline can burn away roadblocks?

How do you think *Tapas* relates to fasting?

Or do you think that is against *ahimsa*?

Describe your yoga practice:

How strong is your focus on your practices? How could you improve your focus?

What sacrifices do you make for practice?

What is spiritual purification to you?

Is your focus on practice constant? Intense?

Are you too intense on your practice?

Does it ever hurt you or others?

How is determination necessary?

Are you enthusiastic about the spiritual path? Does your practice help you have a joyful inner life?

Does your practice feel like a punishment?

Do you think practice has to be hard? Do you think only doing hard poses are real practice?

Do you compare yourself to others, thinking they are more disciplined?

Are you in stillness or suffering each day?

Do you think all difficult things are automatically good?

Do you realize that mastering really difficult poses causes its own set of problems?

The advanced practice means experiencing pleasant and unpleasant emotions and events in your life with awareness and discipline. How are you advanced?

What do you think about this? What is your understanding of the topic now? Draw or write a prayer, poem, affirmation, picture or song lyrics that sums it all up for you.

Self-Study (Svadhyaya)

Svadhyaya is self-study. For very serious yogis, study of the *vedas* (yogic texts) is part of the yoga practice. Modern yogis include the study of great texts and literature from around the globe. The personal discipline *svadhyaya* begins with learning and ends with living an inspired life.

Do you study sacred books and great literature?

What set of scriptures or ancient texts do you like to study?

Has this changed over time? What do you always go back to?

What makes sense to you today?

What are the books of scripture you would take home from a free bookstore?

What is an example of your daily study?

How is your memory when it comes to scripture?

Do you study daily? How? What do you do when you do not understand?

Where do you go or who do you turn to for clarification of something you don't understand?

American Yoga just says "Study" or self-study; what does this mean to you?

Do you think there should be a particular set of scripture to study for yogis and those in yoga teacher training?

What does an atheist yogi study?

How do you meditate on your studies?

Do things just pop up in your mind through the day?

Is it easier to reflect on the big issues in life when you are washing the dishes or doing mindless work?

This practice includes not judging yourself harshly and modeling inspiring people. Describe your models and mentors.

The advanced practice involves being an inspirational person to others and living in balance. Describe how you inspire other people.

What is your understanding of the topic now? Draw or write a prayer, poem, affirmation, picture or song lyrics that sums it all up for you

Surrender (Ishvara Pranidhana)

Isvara or *Ishvara* is translated by some scholars as "a metaphysical concept that is the true self or unchanging self". *Pranidhana* is contemplation, or meditation. So this *niyama* is about contemplation or meditation on the true self, the divine self, or some would say God.

What is the true self? What is the unchanging self?

What is the divinity within?

What is contemplation?

How is it different than meditation?

Have you ever had God or a higher power fully occupy your mind?

What do you think pure consciousness is?

What do you think peace feels like?

What is pure, or total, peace?

The personal discipline *ishvara-pranidhana*, can include surrender, sacrifice and giving. Is a higher power important?

What does surrender mean to you?

How does it feel to fully surrender? What does full surrender look like?

Some say this *niyama* is oneness, pulling it all together. What does oneness mean to you?

The advanced practice is selfless service, doing actions that serve others, and a full time letting go into service. It is not always easy, but leads to a life of integrity. What do you think? Do you agree?

What is your understanding of the topic now? Draw or write a prayer, poem, affirmation, picture or song lyrics that sums it all up for you.

The Third Limb: Yoga Postures

The third limb represents the physical yoga postures we practice for physical flexibility and strength. This section lists groups of yoga poses and leaves room for you to write or draw notes about the pose. You can also use this space to keep track of your progress with each pose or how you like to practice this pose (hot, *vinyasa*, flow, static). Some people like to draw, collage, doodle, color or make stick figure drawings here.

Gentle Standing Poses

Mountain Pose (*Tadasana*)

Tall Mountain or Raised Hands Pose (*Urdhva Hastasana*)

Crescent Moon or C-curve

Five Pointed Star

Standing Spinal Twist (*Sama Matsyendrasana*)

Standing Forward Bend (*Uttanasana*)

Gentle Standing Back Bend (*Anuvittasana*)

Gentle Chair (*Utkatasana*)

Gentle Wide Leg Forward Bend (*Prasarita Padottanasana*)

Supported Pyramid or Intense Side Stretch (*Parsvottanasana*)

Gentle Triangle (*Utthita Trikonasana*)

Gentle Revolved Triangle (*Parivrtta Trikonasana*)

Crescent Lunge (*Alanasana* is sometimes used)

Low Lunge (*Anjaneyasana*)

Warrior I (*Virabhadrasana I*)

Warrior II (*Virabhadrasana II*)

Reverse Warrior (*Viparita Virabhadrasana*)

Gentle Extended Side Angle (*Utthita Parsvakonasana*)

Gentle Balance Poses

Half Moon (*Ardha Chandrasana*)

Warrior III (*Virabhadrasana III*)

Tree (*Vrksasana*)

Dancer (King Dancer Pose – *Natarajasana*)

Hand to Big Toe (*Utthita Hasta Padangusthasana*)

Eagle Pose (*Garudasana*)

Gentle Prone Poses

Table Pose (*Utpithikasana*)

Cat (*Marjaryasana*)

Cow (*Bitilasana*)

Spinal Balance

Classic Child's Pose (*Balasana*)

Runner's Lunge (*Alanasana* is sometimes used)

Plank (*Kumbhakasana*)

Half Plank (*Ardha Kumbhakasana*)

Dolphin Plank (*Makara Adho Mukha Svanasana*)

Half Dolphin Plank (*Makara Adho Mukha Savasana*)

Down Dog (*Adho Mukha Svanasana*)

Upward Facing Dog (*Urdhva Mukha Svanasana*)

Cobra (*Bujangasana*)

Sphinx (*Salamba Bhujangasana*)

Full Locust (*Shalabasana*)

Half Locust (*Ardha Shalabasana*)

One Leg King Pigeon Pose (*Eka Pada Rajakapotasana*)

Extended Child's Pose (*Balasana*)

Restorative Child's Pose (*Balasana*)

Sun Salutation

Moon Salutation

Gentle Seated and Twisting Postures

Easy Seated Pose (*Sukhaasana*)

Staff Pose (*Dandasana*)

Cow Face Pose (*Gomukhasana*)

Gentle Hero Pose (*Virasana*)

Seated Forward Bend (*Paschimottanasana*)

Head to Knee (*Janu Sirsasana*)

Bound Angle (*Baddha Konasana*)

Progressive Seated Twist (*Ardha Matsyendrasana I, II, III*)

Seated Wide Angle Forward Bend (*Upavistha Konasana*)

Upward Boat (*Navasana*)

Gentle Supine Poses and Backbends

Knees to Chest (*Apanasana*)

Reclining Big Toe (*Supta Padangusthasana*)

Reclining Bound Angle (*Supta Badda Konasana*)

Supine Spinal Twist (*Jathara Parivartanasana*)

Gentle Fish (*Matsyasana*)

Bridge and Supported Bridge (*Setu Banda Sarvangasana*)

Gentle Inversions

Happy Baby (*Ananda Balasana*)

Dead Bug (*Matkunasana*)

Half Shoulder Stand (*Arha Salamba Sarvangasana*)

Legs up the Wall (*Viparita Karani*)

Relaxation or Corpse Pose (*Savasana*)

The Fourth Limb: Energy of Life

The fourth limb, *pranayama*, involves breathing techniques, but is also a doorway to the higher meditation practices in yoga. *Pranayama* is the link between the physical and mental disciplines. It is well designed to calm the mind. I often refer to it as a bridge to those functions we do not have conscious control of and the higher states of meditation.

In yoga, the breath is known as *prana* and is considered universal energy that can be used to find a balance between the body-mind. You use breathing techniques to change subtle energies within the body for health.

The breath is used to communicate between systems and it is the only bodily function that we do both voluntarily and involuntarily. We can consciously use breathing to influence the involuntary systems (sympathetic nervous system) that regulates blood pressure, heart rate, circulation, digestion and many other bodily functions.

When did you first begin to practice breath awareness?

When is your primary focus on the breath? When is relaxation secondary?

What happens when you watch breath go in and out of your nostrils?

If you take a deep breath and sigh it out, we call this a cleansing breath. In kid's yoga I call it the "Mommy Breath" because all the kids know what that means. Describe how this breathing technique helps you.

If you lay on your bed and breathe normally while you relax, we call this the Resting breath (this is the one I call "Baby Breath" because you breathe like a baby in a crib)?

When are you not aware of your breath?

If you take a deep breath and allow your belly to expand, we call this abdominal breathing or diaphragmatic breathing. How does it feel if you do this?

Do you feel like you are sometimes a "chest breather"?

When do you feel rapid, shallow, chest breathing?

How do you breathe when you are under stress?

Describe the difference between breathing when you are stresses and breathing when you are relaxed.

What technique helps you focus on the moment?

If you are interested in more information about technique, Google the following techniques and journal about your experience:

Ujjayi Breath,

Ujjayi Cleansing Breath,

Dirga Pranayama or 3-Part Breath

Bellows Breath (*Bastrika*)

Alternate Nostril Breathing (*Anuloma Viloma*)

HAH Breath

Victory Goddess Salute and Breath to Fortify the Nerves

Breath Retention

Skull Shining Breath (*Kapalabhati*)

Kundalini Victory Breath

Mountain Breath

Bumble Bee Breath (*Brahmari*)

Cooling Breath (*Sitkari*)

Straw Breath (*Sithali*)

3 *Bandhas*: *Jalandhara, Uddiyana, Moola Bandha*

What do you think about this? What is your understanding of the topic now? Draw or write a prayer, poem, affirmation, picture or song lyrics that sums it all up for you.

The Fifth Limb: Withdrawal

The last four limbs are gateways to deeper and more profound meditation. The fifth limb, *pratyahara*, means to withdrawal from the senses or transcend them. What does withdrawal from the senses mean to you?

What does transcend the senses mean to you?

List everything that distracts you.

Do you find it difficult to walk away from your cell phone, computer, TV or other devices?

Describe the distraction that is hardest to walk away from.

Describe your experience with meditation.

Describe your favorite guided meditation (if you have one).

Describe your favorite body scan meditations.

Describe the squeeze and relax type meditations.

Describe your experiences with *Yoga Nidra*.

What is the best way for you to unplug?

Imagine you had a slight hearing loss, how would that help you unplug from the world?

Describe a person who can put away all their technological devices and not feel the pull to run back and turn them on until the next day (or week).

Describe a time you got very cold during meditation.

Describe a time you felt pain in meditation.

In my old yoga studio there was a clock on the wall that seemed to me to tick very loudly during my meditation and it drove me crazy at first. Describe something that drives you crazy in mediation.

Describe the process of moving beyond these distractions.

Write about the best meditation experience you ever had and how often this happens for you.

What do you think about this? What is your understanding of the topic now? Draw or write a prayer, poem, affirmation, picture or song lyrics that sums it all up for you.

The Sixth Limb: Concentration

The last three limbs of yoga are deeper and progressively more profound meditation experiences. The sixth limb, *dharana*, means to focus on an object such as a candle flame or the third eye during meditation. Describe your experience with focus. Do you feel like you are focused?

What problems do you have with focus?

List some things that help you focus.

Describe things that help you concentrate.

If you are an extrovert, do other people help you focus?

If you are an introvert, does alone time help you focus?

Are you able to settle your mind on one thing?

What are your favorite objects to focus on in yoga? Draw your favorite objects of focus?

List all the things that bring you out of focus.

Do you have any health, medication or mental health issues that affect your focus?

How can you improve your focus?

Describe your experience with any of the following object of focus:

Mala Beads

Crystal Bowls

Music

Candle Flame

Mantra

List the best yoga poses for focus.

How would you describe the difference between focus and concentration?

When you think about concentration, how does it make you feel?

Tell about a meditation experience where you were instructed to focus on an object.

What do you think about this? What is your understanding of the topic now? Draw or write a prayer, poem, affirmation, picture or song lyrics that sums it all up for you.

The Seventh Limb: Meditation

Meditation, *Dhyana,* is different than the sixth limb, concentration, because we let go of the object of meditation. Now there is a lack of focus. You no longer need an object of meditation. You let go of concentration and slip into meditation.

What happens to you in meditation?

Do you have mind chatter or monkey mind?

How do you deal with mind chatter?

Write the date of your meditation and describe the journey you went on.

What happens to you in deep meditation? Is the mind chatter gone?

Write the date of a different meditation and describe the journey you went on. Compare it to the first one you wrote about. Repeat this as often as you like.

What do you think about this? What is your understanding of the topic now? Draw or write a prayer, poem, affirmation, picture or song lyrics that sums it all up for you.

The Eighth Limb: Bliss

You learned to focus, you can concentrate, you moved to meditation but did you ever feel like time disappeared? The eighth limb is pure peace. Some people believe this is a goal but I tend to think of it as grace.

What does peace feel like?

Describe bliss for you.

List all the things you believe about peace inside yourself.

Write or draw grace.

Let's talk about love. What does love feel like?

What does perfect joy feel like in your life?

What do you think about this? Do you think the yogis have a good and structured plan for peace on earth?

What do you think about the 8 limbs all together as a lifestyle?

Do you think anything is missing in the 8 limb philosophy?

How does the 8 limb system compare to other systems you are familiar with?

What is your understanding of the 8 limbs now? Draw or write a prayer, poem, affirmation, picture or song lyrics that sums up the 8 limbs for you.

About the Author

Beth Daugherty, MS, MA, E-RYT, RCYT. Beth is the founder of Lifespan Yoga®, Director of Teacher Training, and author of the Lifespan Yoga® Books. She has lived in three different yoga centers and trained with a variety of teachers since the early 1980s. In addition to yoga, she has conducted social science research and taught undergraduate research design, statistics, psychology, and program evaluation. Visit www.LifespanYoga.com for more information.

Other Books by Beth Daugherty:

Nikita's Sun (2012)

Lifespan Yoga®: Developmental Psychology Meets the Practice and Teaching of Yoga (2014)

Gentle Yoga: A Lifespan Yoga® Introduction (2015)

Chair Yoga: Lifespan Yoga® for Health and Wellness (2015)

Training and Certifications

Yoga Teacher Training (YTT 200 hour)

The Lifespan Yoga® 200-hour YTT is an excellent opportunity for students motivated to take their gentle yoga practice to the next level or begin teaching yoga. Trainees can expect a heavy emphasis on meditation and deep relaxation.

Kids Yoga Teacher Certification

The 95-hour Lifespan Yoga® Kids and Teen teacher training is for people who want to teach yoga to children and teens. You will learn to incorporate games, art, stories, music, character education, plus age-appropriate meditation to make relaxation creative and fun.

Chair Yoga Teacher Certification

The certification is for anyone who would like to go deeper into a form of yoga that brings the floor up to the student. The training includes learning postures on (or around) chairs, teaching tips for newcomers, and relaxation in chairs.

Gentle Yoga Advanced Training

This training is for anyone who would like to go deeper into the practice of gentle yoga. Current yoga teachers are welcome to take this to brush up on gentle yoga and meditation teaching skills. The training includes focus on the 8 limbs of yoga.

Made in the USA
Lexington, KY
05 July 2018